Lifestyle BLOG Planner
journal

Kaylee Berry

Weston Tree Publishing

Dedication

To all my lifestyle bloggers.
May you have success in all you write, create,
plan and propose.
I look forward to reading all that comes out of your journal.

Table of Contents

HOW TO USE THIS BOOK

Reader Profile

Use the reader profile to get to know your ideal audience. Fill in every blank to create a complete guide of who your readers are, what they like, and what they want from you.

Writing Tips

Read over the tips in this section often to keep your writing interesting and engaging. It will help you to focus on your readers as you write and therefore create better content.

One Year - One Post a Week Schedule

For most blogs one post a week is enough. Use this one-year planner to come up with a theme for each month. Then plan your posts out for each week. For your convenience 5 weeks are included in case you post on a certain day of the week and there happen to be 5 in a month. You will be able to see a whole years worth of content at a glance.

Post Publishing Checklist

Use this helpful checklist every time you get ready to publish a new post. It has all the steps you need to successfully launch a new post. As a bonus there is an additional checklist of extra ways to create more content using your post.

Journal Pages

Use this journal to collect all your *never-ending* ideas. There is room to write about ways to grow your blog, products to launch, and ideas for posts. If you're ever stuck use the prompts to inspire you. In this section of the book you'll also find inspirational quotes to keep you motivated to write, grow your blog, and find success.

Index

Every journal entry has a place to fill in a category. This will allow you to easily categorize your ideas for quick reference later. The index has room for thirteen categories and room enough to write every page number that corresponds with that idea.

IN ORDER TO
HAVE AN AUDIENCE,
YOU MUST WRITE FOR ONE.

-Kaylee Berry

IDEAL READER PROFILE

Name: _____

Age: _____

Location: _____

Occupation: _____

Relationship Status: _____

Religious Preferences: _____

Hobbies: _____

_____

Interests: _____

_____

What are they looking to gain from your blog?_____

_____

_____

What do they spend time online doing? _____

_____

_____

What is their primary need or concern in life? _____

_____

_____

IDEAL READER PROFILE CONT.

Describe their general disposition and personality: _____

_____

_____

_____

What activities would fill their calendar for the next year? _____

_____

_____

_____

What influences their buying decisions? _____

_____

What would make them trust and respect you? _____

_____

_____

Would they ever spend money on services/products you offer? _____

_____

_____

What would it take for them to purchase them from you? _____

_____

_____

What questions would they ask you if they sat across from you drinking coffee? _____

_____

_____

_____

_____

_____

THREE QUESTIONS

Ask yourself these questions before you start writing....

Question 1: What am I writing about?

Choose a theme and main topic. Don't try to cram too many things in a single post. Have no more than two sub-points. Otherwise, it will be hard for your readers to follow along.

Question 2: What am I trying to say?

Know which side of the argument you are on. Choose a simple statement that you can easily remember. Write it down next to your workspace and refer to it often. It will be what you base every writing decision on. Think of it as your worldview.

Ex. I believe all people have the right to work at a job that they love.

Ex. Everyone can live an active lifestyle no matter their age.

Use your "writers statement" to build all of your content. It will be what you are known for.

Question 3: Who am I writing for?

Imagine your ideal reader every time you form a sentence. Think about how they will receive your words. Try to give them what they want. Entertain them, inspire them, move them to have strong emotions, or whatever your goal is in your writing.

Writing Tips

Put Your Readers First

In order to have an audience, you must write for one. You must think about your reader with every word you write. Picture them receiving your ideas, being entertained by your words, finding inspiration in your stories.

Your audience is your number one priority when you write. Whether you're trying to get your reader to spend some of their hard earned money on your book, trying to teach them something, or sharing your experiences to help others going through a similar situation, you must build trust.

They need to know that you have their best interests at heart. They are looking for someone who is genuine and sharing something that interests them. Your audience wants to be entertained, taught, and inspired. Be the kind of writer that delivers what they want.

Be a Thought Leader

The key to having raving fans is to have killer content. Every word out of your mouth should be prophetic.

Your focus should be on producing something that is life changing to anyone who reads it. Filler and fluff just won't cut it. Use your words to inspire others, and they will inspire others with your words.

When you hear or see something amazing, you want to share it with everyone you know. Your following may start out small, but it will grow over time by people sharing what you say.

It takes more than just experience to be a thought leader. It takes stepping out of the norm and thinking outside of the box. It's a combination of mastery and continual searching. There is still much to be discovered. Be a pioneer. Then report back to everyone the wonderful things you've found.

Show Your Audience You're a Real Person

Let your readers get to know the real you. Tell them stories from your life to help them connect with you. Share your struggles and joys.

Bring your personality to whatever you're writing. Don't hide behind your keyboard and create a persona that doesn't represent you. Use words that you would use in everyday conversation. Slip in a bit of your sense of humor.

Give your readers permission to talk to you directly. In fact, ask them to. At the end of posts or emails, encourage them to respond directly to you. If people like you and get to know you, they will trust you.

Write Like You're Talking to a Friend

Picture yourself dialoguing with your best friend or your ideal reader. Use words and phrases you would use in real conversations. Let the conversation flow from one topic to the next.

When you are with a friend, you're not nervous or self-conscious. You are at ease and feel safe. Your writing should convey those things. Show your readers you are comfortable with them.

Open up to them and let them know your secrets. Create inside jokes that only your readers will understand. You want to build community among the people you write for. They will sense your authenticity and be drawn to you and your work.

Share Your Unique Perspective

You may be thinking to yourself, "There are already a ton of blogs out there. Why would anyone want to read mine?" I personally think there could never be enough blogs. Every writer has their own voice and style that is different from any other. What speaks to one person won't have the same effect on the next. That is why the world needs your voice, to reach others like you.

Whatever interests you, most likely interests other people too. So share your unique perspective, and you will find *your* people. Your distinct approach and knowledge on a specific subject will be unique and put you above the rest.

Make It Interesting

Facts and figures are necessary for some audiences. I understand that, but if you don't make your content interesting and lively readers will pass over your work.

Use things we've talked about like personal stories, your unique take on things, writing like you're talking with a friend, using plain language, adding a bit of your humor.

You can break up text with quote or pictures to make your posts more reader-friendly and break up the large sections of text. Doing this will help to keep your readers attention.

Find Your Voice

Decide how you want to present your information. Are you going to be funny and humorous, sarcastic and snarky, gentle and kind, motherly, edgy? You decide what writing style best fits your personality and include it in every piece you write.

This will be your voice.

Final Thoughts

Writing to influence people can be a big responsibility so always aim to encourage and uplift and don't use your words to tear down.

When you think you've run out of ideas and inspiration for writing, commit to journaling every day. You'll be amazed at the thoughts you have when you give yourself some room to breathe and be creative.

ONE YEAR

ONE POST A

WEEK PLANNER

One Year
One Post a Week Schedule

Month:_____ Theme:_____

Post 1   _____
Post 2   _____
Post 3   _____
Post 4   _____
Post 5   _____

Month:_____ Theme:_____

Post 1   _____
Post 2   _____
Post 3   _____
Post 4   _____
Post 5   _____

Month:_____ Theme:_____

Post 1   _____
Post 2   _____
Post 3   _____
Post 4   _____
Post 5   _____

Month:_____ Theme:_____

Post 1   _____
Post 2   _____
Post 3   _____
Post 4   _____
Post 5   _____

Month _November_ Theme: _Family/Gratitude_
Post 1 _What I'm most thankful for_ EXAMPLE
Post 2 _10 Ways to Cultivate Gratitude_

Month:_____ Theme:_____

Post 1 _____
Post 2 _____
Post 3 _____
Post 4 _____
Post 5 _____

Month:_____ Theme:_____

Post 1 _____
Post 2 _____
Post 3 _____
Post 4 _____
Post 5 _____

Month:_____ Theme:_____

Post 1 _____
Post 2 _____
Post 3 _____
Post 4 _____
Post 5 _____

Month:_____ Theme:_____

Post 1 _____
Post 2 _____
Post 3 _____
Post 4 _____
Post 5 _____

Month:_____ Theme:_____

Post 1 _____
Post 2 _____
Post 3 _____
Post 4 _____
Post 5 _____

Month:_____ Theme:_____

Post 1 _____
Post 2 _____
Post 3 _____
Post 4 _____
Post 5 _____

Month:_____ Theme:_____

Post 1 _____
Post 2 _____
Post 3 _____
Post 4 _____
Post 5 _____

Month:_____ Theme:_____

Post 1 _____
Post 2 _____
Post 3 _____
Post 4 _____
Post 5 _____

PUBLISHING CHECKLIST & HEADLINE TEMPLATES

Post Publishing Checklist

☐ Good Title that builds interest

☐ Researched

☐ Proofread

☐ Grammar Checked

☐ Tags added

☐ Link to Old Posts

☐ Add Feature Image

☐ Use Short Paragraphs

☐ Break up the text with Images

☐ Built in SEO (Search Engine Optimization)

☐ Call to Action

☐ Pull out quotes

☐ Highlight or Bold Important Sections for easy Skimming

☐ Share on Social Media Outlets

Create More Content by Re-purposing your Post

☐ Create a video

☐ Use it for a Podcast

☐ Turn it into a series

☐ Use it in a book

☐ Create a workbook/checklist/template

☐ Use the idea to create an E-Course

Blog Post Title/Headline Templates

(#) Things to do on a _____ (particular type of day ex. rainy day)

(#) Reasons you need to Buy _____ (your favorite product)

Your Holiday Wish List

The Do's and Don'ts of _____

Think you know how to _____

How to Start a _____

(#) Habits of Highly Successful _____ (your occupation)

The Do's and Don'ts of _____

(#) Ways to Find Purpose in _____

How to get rid of _____ (something you've mastered or overcome)

Practical Guide to _____

Like _____? Then you'll Love This

Around the house. My favorite things

(#) Inspirational Quotes to _____

What's on my desk? (#) Essential Office Supplies

(#) Things to do This _____ (season)

(#) Steps to a _____ (ex. Joyful) Morning (your morning routine)

Inspiration for _____ (your favorite hobby)

(#) _____(ex. photos, cats, videos) to Lift your Mood

My Favorite Place to _____

_____

_____

Share

your experiences with this blog planner
on social media.

#TheBlogThatNeverEnds

Title: _____

Date   /   /

Category: _____

What happened to me today that would be interesting/entertaining for my readers?

Notes: _____

☐Drafted   ☐Proofread   ☐Published

Title: _____

Category: _____

Date   /   /

Title: _____

Category: _____

Am I learning a lesson or using one I previously learned today?

_____
_____
_____
_____
_____
_____
_____
_____
_____
_____
_____
_____
_____
_____

Notes:_____
_____
_____
_____
_____
_____
_____
_____
_____
_____
_____
_____

☐Drafted   ☐Proofread   ☐Published

Title: _____

Category: _____

Date   /   /

WORDS ARE THE

MEDIUM BY

WHICH WRITERS

CREATE.

-Kaylee Berry

Title: _____

Category:_____

What is something about myself that I've never shared with my readers before?

_____
_____
_____
_____
_____
_____
_____
_____
_____
_____
_____
_____

Notes:_____
_____
_____
_____
_____
_____
_____
_____
_____
_____

28   ☐Drafted   ☐Proofread   ☐Published

Title: _____

Category: _____

Date   /   /

Title: _____

Category: _____

What is on my mind today that I can't stop thinking about?

_____

_____

_____

_____

_____

_____

_____

_____

_____

_____

_____

_____

Notes: _____

_____

_____

_____

_____

_____

_____

_____

_____

☐Drafted   ☐Proofread   ☐Published

Title: _____

Category: _____

Date   /   /

> A POSITIVE
> ATTITUDE CAUSES
> A CHAIN REACTION
> OF POSITIVE
> THOUGHTS, EVENTS
> AND OUTCOMES.
> IT IS A CATALYST
> AND IT SPARKS
> EXTRAORDINARY
> RESULTS.
> *-Wade Boggs*

Title: _____

Category: _____

Date   /   /

Why did I start writing my blog in the first place?

_____
_____
_____
_____
_____
_____
_____
_____
_____
_____
_____
_____
_____
_____

Notes:_____
_____
_____
_____
_____
_____
_____
_____
_____
_____
_____

☐Drafted   ☐Proofread   ☐Published

Title: _____

Date   /   /

Category: _____

Title: _____

Category: _____

What experience did I have today that my audience would like to hear about?

_____
_____
_____
_____
_____
_____
_____
_____
_____
_____
_____
_____
_____
_____

Notes: _____
_____
_____
_____
_____
_____
_____
_____
_____
_____
_____
_____

☐Drafted   ☐Proofread   ☐Published

Title: _____

Category: _____

> SUCCESS IS NO ACCIDENT. IT IS HARD WORK, PERSEVERANCE, LEARNING, STUDYING, SACRIFICE AND MOST OF ALL, LOVE OF WHAT YOU ARE DOING OR LEARNING TO DO.
>
> -Pele

Title: _____   Date   /   /

Category: _____

Why do I love blogging?

Notes: _____

☐Drafted   ☐Proofread   ☐Published

Title: _____

Category: _____

Date _____ / _____ / _____

Title: _____

Category: _____

What is something new I'd like to try?

_____
_____
_____
_____
_____
_____
_____
_____
_____
_____
_____
_____
_____

Notes:_____
_____
_____
_____
_____
_____
_____
_____
_____
_____
_____

☐Drafted   ☐Proofread   ☐Published

Title: _____   Date   /   /

Category: _____

EITHER WRITE
SOMETHING
WORTH
READING OR
DO SOMETHING
WORTH
WRITING.

-*Benjamin Franklin*

Title: _____

Date ___ / ___ / ___

Category: _____

What does my audience want from me?

_____
_____
_____
_____
_____
_____
_____
_____
_____
_____
_____
_____
_____

Notes: _____
_____
_____
_____
_____
_____
_____
_____
_____
_____
_____

40   ☐Drafted   ☐Proofread   ☐Published

Title: _____

Category: _____

Date   /   /

Title: _____   Date   /   /

Category: _____

How can I help to give my readers more of what they are looking for?

_____
_____
_____
_____
_____
_____
_____
_____
_____
_____
_____
_____
_____
_____

Notes: _____
_____
_____
_____
_____
_____
_____
_____
_____
_____
_____
_____
_____

□Drafted   □Proofread   □Published

Title: _____

Category: _____

> I DO NOT SEE THE
> PROCESS OF BLOGGING
> AS A SEPARATE THING
> FROM CREATING ART.
> THIS IS IN PART WHY
> I DO NOT LIKE TO BE
> KNOWN FOR BEING
> A 'BLOGGER,' AS THIS
> IS JUST ONE FORM OF
> OUTPUT FOR CREATIVE
> IDEAS.
>
> *-Keri Smith*

Title: _____

Date   /   /

Category: _____

What is on my bucket list?

_____
_____
_____
_____
_____
_____
_____
_____
_____
_____
_____
_____
_____
_____

Notes: _____
_____
_____
_____
_____
_____
_____
_____
_____
_____
_____

☐Drafted   ☐Proofread   ☐Published

Title: _____

Category: _____

Date   /   /

Title: _____

Date   /   /

Category: _____

Who is my favorite blogger and why?

_____
_____
_____
_____
_____
_____
_____
_____
_____
_____
_____
_____
_____
_____

Notes:_____
_____
_____
_____
_____
_____
_____
_____
_____
_____

☐Drafted   ☐Proofread   ☐Published

Title: _____

Date   /   /

Category: _____

> START WHERE
> YOU ARE. USE
> WHAT YOU
> HAVE. DO WHAT
> YOU CAN.
> *-Arthur Ashe*

Title: _____

Category: _____

How can I learn and grow today?

_____
_____
_____
_____
_____
_____
_____
_____
_____
_____
_____
_____

Notes: _____
_____
_____
_____
_____
_____
_____
_____
_____
_____
_____

☐Drafted   ☐Proofread   ☐Published

Title: _____

Category: _____

Date   /   /

Title: _____   Date   /   /

Category:_____

What is one class I'd like to take?

_____
_____
_____
_____
_____
_____
_____
_____
_____
_____
_____
_____
_____
_____
_____

Notes:_____
_____
_____
_____
_____
_____
_____
_____
_____
_____
_____
_____

☐Drafted   ☐Proofread   ☐Published

Title: _____

Category: _____

_____

_____

_____

_____

_____

_____

_____

_____

_____

_____

_____

_____

_____

_____

_____

_____

> COMMITMENT,
> BELIEF AND POSITIVE
> ATTITUDE ARE
> ALL IMPORTANT
> IF YOU'RE GOING
> TO BE A SUCCESS,
> WHETHER YOU'RE IN
> SPORTS, IN BUSINESS
> OR, AS IN MY CASE,
> ANTHROPOLOGY.
>
> *-Donald Johanson*

☐Drafted   ☐Proofread   ☐Published

Title: _____

Date   /   /

Category: _____

What is my favorite part of being a blogger?

_____
_____
_____
_____
_____
_____
_____
_____
_____
_____
_____
_____
_____
_____

Notes:_____
_____
_____
_____
_____
_____
_____
_____
_____
_____
_____

☐Drafted   ☐Proofread   ☐Published

Title: _____

Category: _____

Date   /   /

Title: _____

Category: _____

What area of blogging do I struggle with most?

_____

_____

_____

_____

_____

_____

_____

_____

_____

_____

_____

_____

_____

Notes: _____

_____

_____

_____

_____

_____

_____

_____

_____

_____

_____

☐Drafted ☐Proofread ☐Published

Title: _____

Category: _____

Date   /   /

YOUR POSITIVE
ACTION
COMBINED
WITH POSITIVE
THINKING
RESULTS IN
SUCCESS.

-Shiv Khera

Title: _____

Category: _____

What advice would I give to my younger self?

_____
_____
_____
_____
_____
_____
_____
_____
_____
_____
_____
_____
_____
_____

Notes:_____
_____
_____
_____
_____
_____
_____
_____
_____
_____
_____
_____

□Drafted   □Proofread   □Published

Title: _____

Category: _____

Date   /   /

Title: _____

Category: _____

What have I read recently that inspired me?

_____
_____
_____
_____
_____
_____
_____
_____
_____
_____
_____
_____
_____

Notes: _____
_____
_____
_____
_____
_____
_____
_____
_____
_____
_____

☐ Drafted   ☐ Proofread   ☐ Published

Title: _____

Category: _____

Date ___ / ___ / ___

HAPPINESS IS NOT
SOMETHING YOU
POSTPONE FOR
THE FUTURE; IT IS
SOMETHING YOU
DESIGN FOR THE
PRESENT.

-Jim Rohn

Title: _____

Category: _____

Date   /   /

How can I help my readers in the areas that they are interested in?

_____
_____
_____
_____
_____
_____
_____
_____
_____
_____
_____
_____
_____

Notes:_____
_____
_____
_____
_____
_____
_____
_____
_____
_____

☐Drafted   ☐Proofread   ☐Published

Title: _____   Date   /   /

Category: _____

_____

_____

_____

_____

_____

_____

_____

_____

_____

_____

_____

_____

_____

_____

_____

_____

_____

_____

_____

_____

_____

_____

_____

_____

☐Drafted   ☐Proofread   ☐Published

Title: _____

Category: _____

Date   /   /

What could I teach my audience?

_____
_____
_____
_____
_____
_____
_____
_____
_____
_____
_____
_____

Notes:_____
_____
_____
_____
_____
_____
_____
_____
_____
_____
_____

    ☐Drafted   ☐Proofread   ☐Published

Title: _____

Category: _____

Date   /   /

> ## SOME PEOPLE DREAM OF SUCCESS, WHILE OTHER PEOPLE GET UP EVERY MORNING AND MAKE IT HAPPEN.
>
> *-Wayne Huizenga*

Title: _____

Category: _____

What is my biggest struggle in life?

_____
_____
_____
_____
_____
_____
_____
_____
_____
_____
_____
_____

Notes: _____
_____
_____
_____
_____
_____
_____
_____
_____
_____

☐Drafted   ☐Proofread   ☐Published

Title: _____   Date   /   /

Category: _____

Title: _____

Category: _____

What do my readers struggle with?

_____
_____
_____
_____
_____
_____
_____
_____
_____
_____
_____
_____

Notes: _____
_____
_____
_____
_____
_____
_____
_____
_____
_____

☐Drafted   ☐Proofread   ☐Published

Title: _____

Category: _____

> HABITS LIKE
> BLOGGING OFTEN AND
> REGULARLY, WRITING
> DOWN THE WAY YOU
> THINK, BEING CLEAR
> ABOUT WHAT YOU
> THINK ARE EFFECTIVE
> TACTICS, IGNORING
> THE BURBLING CROWD
> ...ALL OF THESE ARE
> USEFUL HABITS.
>
> *-Seth Godin*

☐Drafted   ☐Proofread   ☐Published

Title: _____

Category: _____

What marketing ideas do I have for my blog?

Notes: _____

☐Drafted   ☐Proofread   ☐Published

Title: _____

Category: _____

Date   /   /

Title: _____

Category: _____

Date   /   /

What do I want my brand to stand for?

_____
_____
_____
_____
_____
_____
_____
_____
_____
_____
_____
_____
_____

Notes:_____
_____
_____
_____
_____
_____
_____
_____
_____
_____

☐Drafted   ☐Proofread   ☐Published

Title: _____

Category: _____

Date: _____ / _____ / _____

WRITING, TO
ME, IS SIMPLY
THINKING
THROUGH MY
FINGERS.

-Isaac Asimov

Title: _____   Date   /   /

Category: _____

If I were to start another blog what would it be about?

Notes:

❑Drafted   ❑Proofread   ❑Published

Title: _____   Date   /   /

Category: _____

Title: _____

Category: _____

What is my favorite thing to do on the weekend?

_____
_____
_____
_____
_____
_____
_____
_____
_____
_____
_____
_____

Notes: _____
_____
_____
_____
_____
_____
_____
_____
_____
_____

☐Drafted ☐Proofread ☐Published

Title: _____

Date Date   /   /

Category: _____

> YOUR WRITING VOICE
> IS THE DEEPEST
> POSSIBLE REFLECTION
> OF WHO YOU ARE....
> IN YOUR VOICE, YOUR
> READERS SHOULD BE
> ABLE TO HEAR THE
> CONTENTS OF YOUR
> MIND, YOUR HEART,
> YOUR SOUL.
>
> -Meg Rosoff

☐Drafted   ☐Proofread   ☐Published

Title: _____

Category: _____

How can I insert my unique voice and perspective into the article I'm currently working on?

_____
_____
_____
_____
_____
_____
_____
_____
_____
_____
_____
_____
_____
_____

Notes: _____
_____
_____
_____
_____
_____
_____
_____
_____
_____
_____
_____

☐Drafted   ☐Proofread   ☐Published

Title: _____   Date   /   /

Category: _____

Title: _____

Category: _____

Write up a proposal to publish a guest post on your favorite blog?

_____
_____
_____
_____
_____
_____
_____
_____
_____
_____
_____
_____
_____
_____
_____

Notes:_____
_____
_____
_____
_____
_____
_____
_____
_____
_____
_____

☐Drafted   ☐Proofread   ☐Published

Title: _____

Category: _____

> THESE DAYS, YOU
> HAVE THE OPTION
> OF STAYING HOME,
> BLOGGING IN YOUR
> UNDERWEAR, AND
> NOT HAVING YOUR
> WORDS MANGLED.
> I THINK I LIKE THE
> DIRECTION THINGS
> ARE HEADED.
>
> *-Marc Andreessen*

Title: _____

Category: _____

How would I describe myself to someone I've never met?

_____
_____
_____
_____
_____
_____
_____
_____
_____
_____
_____
_____
_____
_____

Notes: _____
_____
_____
_____
_____
_____
_____
_____
_____
_____
_____

☐Drafted   ☐Proofread   ☐Published

Title: _____   Date   /   /

Category: _____

_____

_____

_____

_____

_____

_____

_____

_____

_____

_____

_____

_____

_____

_____

_____

_____

_____

_____

_____

_____

_____

_____

_____

_____

_____

☐Drafted   ☐Proofread   ☐Published

Title: _____

Category: _____

Date _____ / _____ / _____

What skill have I learned that I could pass on to my readers?

_____
_____
_____
_____
_____
_____
_____
_____
_____
_____
_____
_____
_____

Notes:_____
_____
_____
_____
_____
_____
_____
_____
_____
_____
_____
_____

☐Drafted   ☐Proofread   ☐Published

Title: _____

Category: _____

HAPPINESS LIES
IN THE JOY OF
ACHIEVEMENT
AND THE THRILL
OF CREATIVE
EFFORT.

-Franklin D. Roosevelt

Title: _____

Category: _____

Go learn something about blogging today. Then write down what
your biggest takeaways were.

_____
_____
_____
_____
_____
_____
_____
_____
_____
_____
_____
_____
_____
_____

Notes: _____
_____
_____
_____
_____
_____
_____
_____
_____
_____
_____
_____

☐Drafted   ☐Proofread   ☐Published

Title: _____

Category: _____

_____

_____

_____

_____

_____

_____

_____

_____

_____

_____

_____

_____

_____

_____

_____

_____

_____

_____

_____

_____

_____

_____

_____

_____

_____

_____

_____

☐Drafted   ☐Proofread   ☐Published

Title: _____

Category: _____

Date   /   /

Does my branding need updating? Brainstorm ideas below.

_____
_____
_____
_____
_____
_____
_____
_____
_____
_____
_____
_____

Notes:_____
_____
_____
_____
_____
_____
_____
_____
_____

☐Drafted   ☐Proofread   ☐Published

Title: _____   Date   /   /

Category: _____

SUCCESS ISN'T
ALWAYS ABOUT
GREATNESS.
IT'S ABOUT
CONSISTENCY.
CONSISTENT HARD
WORK LEADS TO
SUCCESS. GREATNESS
WILL COME.

-Dwayne Johnson

Title: _____

Category: _____

Tell your readers about your day? Do you have a routine you follow?

_____

_____

_____

_____

_____

_____

_____

_____

_____

_____

_____

_____

_____

Notes: _____

_____

_____

_____

_____

_____

_____

_____

_____

_____

_____

☐Drafted   ☐Proofread   ☐Published

Title: _____

Category: _____

Date   /   /

Title: _____

Category: _____

Visualize your blog being a success. What does that look like to you?

Notes: _____

☐Drafted   ☐Proofread   ☐Published

Title: _____

Category: _____

Date ___ / ___ / ___

> A MILLION AND
> ONE THOUGHTS
> FLY THROUGH MY
> BRAIN EVERY DAY.
> IF I DON'T WRITE
> SOME OF THEM
> DOWN BRILLIANT
> IDEAS COULD BE
> LOST.
>
> -Kaylee Berry

Title: _____ Date   /   /

Category: _____

Who has been a mentor to me and what have they taught me?

_____
_____
_____
_____
_____
_____
_____
_____
_____
_____
_____
_____
_____

Notes: _____
_____
_____
_____
_____
_____
_____
_____
_____
_____
_____

☐ Drafted   ☐ Proofread   ☐ Published

Title: _____

Category: _____

Date   /   /

Title: _____

Category: _____

Date   /   /

What is consuming my thoughts today?

_____
_____
_____
_____
_____
_____
_____
_____
_____
_____
_____
_____
_____

Notes:_____
_____
_____
_____
_____
_____
_____
_____
_____
_____
_____

☐Drafted   ☐Proofread   ☐Published

Title: _____   Date   /   /

Category: _____

> SLOW DOWN AND
> ENJOY LIFE. IT'S
> NOT ONLY THE
> SCENERY YOU MISS
> BY GOING TO FAST -
> YOU ALSO MISS THE
> SENSE OF WHERE
> YOU ARE GOING
> AND WHY.
>
> *-Eddie Cantor*

☐Drafted   ☐Proofread   ☐Published

Title: _____

Category: _____

Date   /   /

What would I like to do a series of blog posts on?

_____
_____
_____
_____
_____
_____
_____
_____
_____
_____
_____
_____
_____

Notes: _____
_____
_____
_____
_____
_____
_____
_____
_____
_____

    ☐Drafted   ☐Proofread   ☐Published

Title: _____

Category: _____

Date   /   /

Title: _____

Category: _____

What is something I would like to do, but feel like it's out of my comfort zone?

_____
_____
_____
_____
_____
_____
_____
_____
_____
_____
_____
_____
_____
_____

Notes: _____
_____
_____
_____
_____
_____
_____
_____
_____
_____
_____
_____

☐Drafted   ☐Proofread   ☐Published

Title: _____

Category: _____

Date ___ / ___ / ___

> PEOPLE TAKE
> DIFFERENT
> ROADS SEEKING
> FULFILLMENT AND
> HAPPINESS. JUST
> BECAUSE THEY'RE
> NOT ON YOUR ROAD
> DOESN'T MEAN
> THEY'VE GOTTEN
> LOST.
>
> -H. Jackson Brown, Jr.

Title: _____

Category: _____

Who would I like to collaborate with on a product or giveaway?

Notes: _____

☐Drafted   ☐Proofread   ☐Published

Title: _____   Date   /   /

Category: _____

Title: _____

Category: _____

Date   /   /

How can I grow my email list this month?

_____
_____
_____
_____
_____
_____
_____
_____
_____
_____
_____
_____
_____

Notes:_____
_____
_____
_____
_____
_____
_____
_____
_____

☐Drafted   ☐Proofread   ☐Published

Title: _____

Category: _____

> SUCCESS IS
> NOT THE KEY
> TO HAPPINESS.
> HAPPINESS IS THE
> KEY TO SUCCESS. IF
> YOU LOVE WHAT
> YOU ARE DOING,
> YOU WILL BE
> SUCCESSFUL.
>
> *-Albert Schweitzer*

☐Drafted   ☐Proofread   ☐Published

Title: _____

Category:_____

What kind of giveaway/freebie could I create to go with my most popular post?

_____
_____
_____
_____
_____
_____
_____
_____
_____
_____
_____
_____
_____
_____

Notes:_____
_____
_____
_____
_____
_____
_____
_____
_____
_____
_____

☐Drafted   ☐Proofread   ☐Published

Title: _____

Category: _____

_____

_____

_____

_____

_____

_____

_____

_____

_____

_____

_____

_____

_____

_____

_____

_____

_____

_____

_____

_____

_____

_____

_____

_____

_____

_____

_____

_____

☐Drafted   ☐Proofread   ☐Published

Title: _____

Category: _____

Is there any affiliate programs I need to check out? List them below.

_____
_____
_____
_____
_____
_____
_____
_____
_____
_____
_____
_____
_____
_____

Notes: _____
_____
_____
_____
_____
_____
_____
_____
_____
_____
_____
_____

☐Drafted   ☐Proofread   ☐Published

Title: _____

Category: _____

Date   /   /

> TO BE YOURSELF
> IN A WORLD THAT
> IS CONSTANTLY
> TRYING TO MAKE
> YOU SOMETHING
> ELSE IS THE GREATEST
> ACCOMPLISHMENT.
>
> *-Ralph Waldo Emerson*

☐Drafted   ☐Proofread   ☐Published

Title: _____

Category: _____

What product or service am I loving right now that I could write a review about?

Notes: _____

☐Drafted ☐Proofread ☐Published

Title: _____

Category: _____

Date   /   /

Title: _____

Category: _____

What can I share with my readers about myself that will make me more relatable?

_____
_____
_____
_____
_____
_____
_____
_____
_____
_____
_____
_____
_____
_____

Notes: _____
_____
_____
_____
_____
_____
_____
_____
_____
_____
_____

☐Drafted   ☐Proofread   ☐Published

Title: _____

Category: _____

Date   /   /

WRITING MEANS
SHARING. IT'S PART
OF THE HUMAN
CONDITION
TO WANT TO
SHARE THINGS -
THOUGHTS, IDEAS,
OPINIONS.

-Paulo Coelho

Title: _____

Category: _____

Date   /   /

What am I thankful for today?

_____

_____

_____

_____

_____

_____

_____

_____

_____

_____

_____

_____

_____

_____

Notes:_____

_____

_____

_____

_____

_____

_____

_____

_____

_____

_____

☐Drafted   ☐Proofread   ☐Published

Title: _____

Category: _____

Date   /   /

Title: _____

Category: _____

Date   /   /

How can I improve my writing productivity?

_____
_____
_____
_____
_____
_____
_____
_____
_____
_____
_____
_____

Notes:_____
_____
_____
_____
_____
_____
_____
_____
_____
_____

☐Drafted   ☐Proofread   ☐Published

Title: _____

Category: _____

> ## THE SECRET OF YOUR SUCCESS IS DETERMINED BY YOUR DAILY AGENDA.
>
> *-John C. Maxwell*

☐Drafted   ☐Proofread   ☐Published

Title: _____

Category: _____

How did I get introduced to my favorite hobby?

_____

_____

_____

_____

_____

_____

_____

_____

_____

_____

_____

_____

_____

Notes: _____

_____

_____

_____

_____

_____

_____

_____

_____

_____

_____

☐Drafted   ☐Proofread   ☐Published

Title: _____   Date   /   /

Category: _____

Title: _____

Category: _____

Date   /   /

Looking back, what is one thing you would do differently and how can you help your readers avoid your mistakes?

_____
_____
_____
_____
_____
_____
_____
_____
_____
_____
_____
_____
_____
_____
_____

Notes:_____
_____
_____
_____
_____
_____
_____
_____
_____
_____
_____

☐Drafted   ☐Proofread   ☐Published

Title: _____

Category: _____

Date   /   /

I INTEND TO

LIVE LIFE, NOT

JUST EXIST.

-George Takei

Title: _____

Category: _____

What is one of your BIG goals? How will you celebrate when you achieve it?

_____
_____
_____
_____
_____
_____
_____
_____
_____
_____
_____
_____
_____
_____
_____

Notes: _____
_____
_____
_____
_____
_____
_____
_____
_____
_____
_____
_____
_____

☐Drafted   ☐Proofread   ☐Published

Title: _____

Category: _____

Date   /   /

Title: _____

Category: _____

Where do you draw inspiration from for your blog?

_____
_____
_____
_____
_____
_____
_____
_____
_____
_____
_____
_____
_____

Notes: _____
_____
_____
_____
_____
_____
_____
_____
_____
_____
_____

☐Drafted   ☐Proofread   ☐Published

Title: _____

Category: _____

Date   /   /

> ALWAYS DO YOUR
> BEST. WHAT YOU
> PLANT NOW, YOU
> WILL HARVEST
> LATER.
>
> *-Og Mandino*

☐Drafted   ☐Proofread   ☐Published

Title: _____

Category: _____

What is my favorite post I've written to date? Could I do a follow up post?

_____

_____

_____

_____

_____

_____

_____

_____

_____

_____

_____

_____

_____

_____

Notes:_____

_____

_____

_____

_____

_____

_____

_____

_____

_____

☐Drafted   ☐Proofread   ☐Published

Title: _____

Category: _____

Date   /   /

Title: _____

Category: _____

What is the best advice I ever got?

Notes: _____

☐Drafted ☐Proofread ☐Published

Title: _____

Category: _____

_____

_____

_____

_____

_____

_____

_____

_____

_____

_____

_____

_____

_____

_____

_____

_____

_____

_____

_____

_____

> BE PATIENT,
> WORK HARD AND
> CONSISTENTLY,
> HAVE FAITH IN
> YOUR WRITING,
> AND DON'T BE
> AFRAID TO LISTEN
> TO CONSTRUCTIVE
> CRITICISM.
>
> *-Jonathan Galassi*

Title: _____

Category:_____

What can I do to show my readers who I really am?

_____
_____
_____
_____
_____
_____
_____
_____
_____
_____
_____
_____
_____
_____

Notes:_____
_____
_____
_____
_____
_____
_____
_____
_____
_____
_____

☐Drafted   ☐Proofread   ☐Published

Title: _____

Category: _____

Date   /   /

Title: _____

Category: _____

Date   /   /

What creative way can I market my blog this week?

_____
_____
_____
_____
_____
_____
_____
_____
_____
_____
_____
_____
_____

Notes:_____
_____
_____
_____
_____
_____
_____
_____
_____
_____
_____
_____

☐Drafted   ☐Proofread   ☐Published

Title: _____

Category: _____

Date   /   /

THE STARTING
POINT OF ALL
ACHIEVEMENT IS
DESIRE.

-Napoleon Hill

Title: _____

Category: _____

What inspired me today?

_____
_____
_____
_____
_____
_____
_____
_____
_____
_____
_____
_____

Notes: _____
_____
_____
_____
_____
_____
_____
_____
_____
_____

☐Drafted   ☐Proofread   ☐Published

Title: _____

Category: _____

Date   /   /

Title: _____

Category: _____

How much effort am I willing to put in to make my blog a success?

_____
_____
_____
_____
_____
_____
_____
_____
_____
_____
_____
_____
_____

Notes: _____
_____
_____
_____
_____
_____
_____
_____
_____
_____
_____
_____

☐Drafted   ☐Proofread   ☐Published

Title: _____ Date   /   /

Category: _____

> THE FUTURE
> BELONGS TO
> THOSE WHO
> BELIEVE IN THE
> BEAUTY OF
> THEIR DREAMS.
>
> *-Eleanor Roosevelt*

Title: _____   Date   /   /

Category: _____

What are my interests and hobbies? Do my readers share the same
interests?

_____
_____
_____
_____
_____
_____
_____
_____
_____
_____
_____
_____
_____

Notes: _____
_____
_____
_____
_____
_____
_____
_____
_____
_____
_____

☐Drafted   ☐Proofread   ☐Published

Title: _____

Category: _____

Date   /   /

Title: _____   Date   /   /

Category: _____

If I could do anything, knowing I wouldn't fail, What would I do?

_____
_____
_____
_____
_____
_____
_____
_____
_____
_____
_____
_____
_____
_____

Notes:_____
_____
_____
_____
_____
_____
_____
_____
_____
_____

☐Drafted   ☐Proofread   ☐Published

Title: _____

Category: _____

I MADE A
DECISION TO
WRITE FOR MY
READERS, NOT
TO TRY TO FIND
MORE READERS
FOR MY WRITING.

-Seth Godin

☐Drafted   ☐Proofread   ☐Published

Title: _____   Date   /   /

Category: _____

What unique experiences have I had in my life that I can share with my audience?

Notes: _____

☐Drafted   ☐Proofread   ☐Published

Title: _____

Category: _____

Date   /   /

Title: _____

Category: _____

What is one question you keep asking yourself? Go do some
research and report back here.

_____

_____

_____

_____

_____

_____

_____

_____

_____

_____

_____

_____

_____

_____

Notes: _____

_____

_____

_____

_____

_____

_____

_____

_____

_____

☐Drafted   ☐Proofread   ☐Published

Title: _____ Date ___ / ___ / ___

Category: _____

OPTIMISM IS THE FAITH THAT LEADS TO ACHIEVEMENT. NOTHING CAN BE DONE WITHOUT HOPE AND CONFIDENCE.

-Helen Keller

Title: _____   Date   /   /

Category: _____

What is one life lesson I had to learn the hard way?

Notes:_____

☐Drafted   ☐Proofread   ☐Published

Title: _____

Category: _____

Date   /   /

Title: _____

Category: _____

Have you ever thought about writing a book? Could you re-purpose parts of your blog to accomplish this?

_____

_____

_____

_____

_____

_____

_____

_____

_____

_____

_____

_____

_____

_____

Notes: _____

_____

_____

_____

_____

_____

_____

_____

_____

_____

_____

_____

☐Drafted   ☐Proofread   ☐Published

Title: _____

Category: _____

> THE DISCIPLINE
> OF WRITING
> SOMETHING
> DOWN IS THE
> FIRST STEP
> TOWARD MAKING
> IT HAPPEN.
>
> *-Lee Iacocca*

Title: _____

Category: _____

What will you promise your blogging community this month and how will you deliver?

_____
_____
_____
_____
_____
_____
_____
_____
_____
_____
_____
_____
_____

Notes:_____
_____
_____
_____
_____
_____
_____
_____
_____
_____

☐Drafted   ☐Proofread   ☐Published

Title: _____

Category: _____

Date   /   /

☐Drafted   ☐Proofread   ☐Published   149

Title: _____

Category: _____

Who is my idol? Describe the conversation you would have if you had the chance to meet in real life.

_____
_____
_____
_____
_____
_____
_____
_____
_____
_____
_____
_____
_____
_____

Notes: _____
_____
_____
_____
_____
_____
_____
_____
_____
_____
_____

☐Drafted   ☐Proofread   ☐Published

Title: _____

Category: _____

WITH THE NEW

DAY COMES NEW

STRENGTH AND

NEW THOUGHTS.

-*Eleanor Roosevelt*

Title: _____   Date   /   /

Category: _____

In what ways can I give back to my community, either online or in person?

Notes:

☐Drafted   ☐Proofread   ☐Published

Title: _____

Category: _____

Date   /   /

Title: _____

Category: _____

Date   /   /

Brainstorm ideas for holiday posts?

Notes:_____

☐Drafted   ☐Proofread   ☐Published

Title: _____

Category: _____

KEEP YOUR EYES

ON THE STARS,

AND YOUR FEET

ON THE GROUND.

-Theodore Roosevelt

☐Drafted   ☐Proofread   ☐Published   155

Title: _____   Date   /   /

Category: _____

What is my favorite book?

Notes:_____

☐Drafted   ☐Proofread   ☐Published

Title: _____

Category: _____

Date   /   /

Title: _____

Category: _____

Do you have a goal setting strategy? If so share it below.

_____
_____
_____
_____
_____
_____
_____
_____
_____
_____
_____
_____
_____

Notes: _____
_____
_____
_____
_____
_____
_____
_____
_____
_____

☐Drafted   ☐Proofread   ☐Published

Title: _____

Category: _____

Date ___ / ___ / ___

> SETTING GOALS
> IS THE FIRST STEP
> IN TURNING THE
> INVISIBLE INTO
> THE VISIBLE.
>
> -Tony Robbins

☐ Drafted   ☐ Proofread   ☐ Published

Title: _____

Category: _____

What type of culture do you want to create around your blog?

_____
_____
_____
_____
_____
_____
_____
_____
_____
_____
_____
_____
_____
_____

Notes: _____
_____
_____
_____
_____
_____
_____
_____
_____
_____
_____

☐Drafted   ☐Proofread   ☐Published

Title: _____

Category: _____

Date   /   /

Title: _____   Date   /   /

Category: _____

How will I attract new readers to my blog?

_____
_____
_____
_____
_____
_____
_____
_____
_____
_____
_____
_____
_____
_____

Notes:_____
_____
_____
_____
_____
_____
_____
_____
_____
_____
_____
_____

☐Drafted   ☐Proofread   ☐Published

Title: _____

Category: _____

DON'T WATCH

THE CLOCK; DO

WHAT IT DOES.

KEEP GOING.

-Sam Levenson

☐Drafted   ☐Proofread   ☐Published

Title: _____

Category: _____

Who are my people? Where do I find them?

_____
_____
_____
_____
_____
_____
_____
_____
_____
_____
_____
_____
_____
_____

Notes:_____
_____
_____
_____
_____
_____
_____
_____
_____
_____
_____
_____
_____

☐Drafted   ☐Proofread   ☐Published

Title: _____

Category: _____

Date   /   /

Title: _____

Category: _____

Date _____ / _____ / _____

Write your best sales pitch for a new product/course you want to create?

_____
_____
_____
_____
_____
_____
_____
_____
_____
_____
_____
_____
_____
_____

Notes:_____
_____
_____
_____
_____
_____
_____
_____
_____
_____
_____

☐Drafted   ☐Proofread   ☐Published

Title: _____

Category: _____

COMMUNICATION
- THE HUMAN
CONNECTION -
IS THE KEY TO
PERSONAL AND
CAREER SUCCESS.

-Paul J. Meyer

Product Reviews

☆☆☆☆☆

Product Name: _____

Company: _____

Thoughts:_____

_____

_____

_____

☆☆☆☆☆

Product Name: _____

Company: _____

Thoughts:_____

_____

_____

_____

☆☆☆☆☆

Product Name: _____

Company: _____

Thoughts:_____

_____

_____

_____

☆☆☆☆☆

Product Name: _____

Company: _____

Thoughts:_____

_____

_____

_____

Product Reviews

☆☆☆☆☆

Product Name: _____

Company: _____

Thoughts:_____

_____

_____

_____

☆☆☆☆☆

Product Name: _____

Company: _____

Thoughts:_____

_____

_____

_____

☆☆☆☆☆

Product Name: _____

Company: _____

Thoughts:_____

_____

_____

_____

☆☆☆☆☆

Product Name: _____

Company: _____

Thoughts:_____

_____

_____

_____

Index

EXAMPLE

Category:_____Finance_____

Pages 4, 16, 54, 60 _____

_____

Category:_____

Pages _____

_____

_____

Category:_____

Pages _____

_____

_____

Category:_____

Pages _____

_____

_____

Category:_____

Pages _____

_____

_____

Category:_____

Pages _____

_____

_____

Category:_____

Pages _____

_____

_____

_____

Category:_____

Pages _____

_____

_____

_____

Category:_____

Pages _____

_____

_____

_____

Category:_____

Pages _____

_____

_____

_____

Category:_____

Pages _____

_____

_____

_____

Category:_____

Pages _____

_____

_____

_____

Category:_____

Pages _____

_____

_____

_____

Category:_____

Pages _____

_____

_____

_____

About the Author

Who is Kaylee?
Kaylee always wanted to be a writer when she grew up, and now a lifelong dream has come true. She is a self-published author her first book in 2016. The title is "New Baby, New You" It's a book about resolutions to help the new mom.

Kaylee has been keeping a journal and writing in a diary since the first grade. She enjoys writing short stories and now, writing on self-help topics which is another one of her passions. She's always trying to learn and grow and wants to help others do the same.

She was home schooled, along with her brother, which allowed her the freedom to start her small handmade invitation business, Kards by Kaylee, when she was just 17 years old.

She is married to her high school sweetheart, and they have started a family together. She is the mother of a fiery little redhead. She is thankful for a hardworking husband who provides for their family so that she can continue to work from home.

Having always been goal-oriented, entrepreneurial, and continuously reading self-help books, she is a wealth of knowledge. Her goal is to inspire people with her words.

You can find her blog at www.kayleeberry.com and follow along with her latest writing projects.

"I'm excited to grow my following and help other bloggers along the way." –Kaylee

Writing Habit Creation Online Training Course

Take Control of Your Future and Get the Tools You Need to Achieve Your Dreams… And Increase Your Writing Productivity.

Are you like I was…struggling to find time to write and balancing family life. Do you have so many ideas for books or blog posts you're about to burst if you don't get them out? Are you looking to earn income writing part-time but are finding it hard to fit everything in a day? Do you want to write full time but lack the productivity you need to get everything done?

In this NEW Training, you will discover...

- Your "Why" for wanting to write so you can overcome any obstacle
- How to fit writing into your busy schedule
- Even spare moments can fuel your habit
- How to double or even triple your daily word count
- That you can build a daily habit that will stick
- How to always have inspiration
- The best way to reward your self and fuel your new habit
- How to reach your writing goals
- My 4-Step process to create any habit plus the tools to help you along the way
- And More!

Your message—your story–matters. Somebody is out there waiting for it. But if you don't have time to get your message out there into the world, it's not doing anybody and good… least of all you and your bank account.

Start creating the habit of writing everyday now!

http://kayleeberry.com/i-resolve-to-write/

TITLES IN THE SERIES "THE BLOG THAT NEVER ENDS"

Available Now

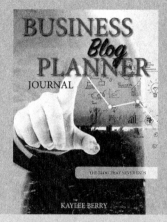

Available January 2018

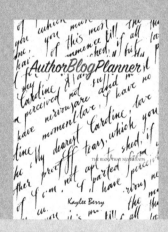

Minimalist Blog Planner Journal	DIY Blog Planner Journal	Fitness Blog Planner Journal

CPSIA information can be obtained
at www.ICGtesting.com
Printed in the USA
FSOW03n1456181217
42560FS